Original title:
The Dreamcatcher's Tale

Copyright © 2025 Swan Charm

Author: Linda Leevike
ISBN HARDBACK: 978-9908-1-4888-5
ISBN PAPERBACK: 978-9908-1-4889-2
ISBN EBOOK: 978-9908-1-4890-8

Threads of Luminescence

In the quiet glow of night,
Stars weave dreams, soft and bright.
Fleeting wisps of silver light,
Guide our hopes, take our flight.

Whispers dance on gentle air,
Carrying secrets, light as prayer.
Each thread spun with tender care,
A tapestry beyond compare.

Through the dark, they twinkle fair,
Filling hearts, chasing despair.
In their warmth, we're not aware,
Of the shadows that they bear.

Shattered pieces start to blend,
In the night, we learn to mend.
Threads entwined, they never end,
A cosmic dream, a timeless friend.

As horizons start to glow,
With dawn's soft, awakening show.
Threads of light begin to flow,
Carving paths where wanderers go.

Silhouettes in the Moonlight

Beneath the stars, shadows play,
Silhouettes in bright array.
Dancing softly, night's ballet,
Whispering secrets, come what may.

Branches sway in soft surrender,
Moonbeams cast, a glowing render.
Figures shrouded, sweet and tender,
Drawing closer, hearts grow fonder.

Echoes of laughter gently sigh,
Flickering flames, night's lullaby.
In the stillness, moments fly,
As dreams take wing and dare to fly.

Waves of silver kiss the ground,
Lost in silence, magic found.
Silhouettes in love, unbound,
In the night, our hopes resound.

As dawn peeks with gentle grace,
We'll hold these memories in space.
Silhouettes in time, embrace,
Forever etched, our sacred place.

Moonlit Confessions

Under the silver glow,
Whispers rise and fall,
Secrets dance like shadows,
In the night's soft call.

Hearts laid bare and free,
Beneath the watchful moon,
Each truth a gentle breeze,
Hums a wistful tune.

Stars blink in silent trust,
As dreams begin to weave,
In this sacred hush,
We learn to truly believe.

Time drips like candle wax,
Moments melt away,
In the night we find strength,
To face the coming day.

A sigh slips through the dark,
Binds the broken seams,
Here in this moonlit space,
We stitch our fragile dreams.

Threads of Memory

Worn photographs in hand,
Fingers trace the past,
Echoes linger softly,
In shadows that we cast.

Laughter rings like church bells,
Amongst the faded trees,
Every smile a thread spun,
In life's vast tapestry.

Scent of rain on pavement,
Brings back forgotten days,
Moments sewn together,
In the heart's warm haze.

Whispers of old secrets,
Float through summer air,
In the quiet garden,
Memories bloom and share.

Every thread a story,
Woven tight and strong,
In the fabric of our lives,
Where we all belong.

Lucid Reflections

Mirrors hold the journey,
Fragments of our dreams,
In every crisp reflection,
The spirit softly gleams.

Waves of thought dance gently,
Under the sun's bright gaze,
Ripples in the surface,
Guide us through the maze.

Clarity emerges slow,
As mist begins to clear,
With each step toward the light,
Our purpose draws near.

Voices echo within,
Wisdom from the past,
In the stillness, we find,
Truths we thought would last.

Bathed in golden sunlight,
Hope unfurls its wings,
Every lucid moment,
A symphony that sings.

Gossamer Journeys

Wings of fragile whispers,
Soar on morning breeze,
Chasing dreams of daylight,
Amongst the rustling leaves.

Paths of silver moonlight,
Guide the wandering feet,
Every turn revealing,
Secrets bittersweet.

A dance upon the dawn,
Where shadows blend with light,
Gossamer threads of time,
Hold the day and night.

Across the fields of gold,
Adventures pulse and play,
In every heart's desire,
Lies a brand new day.

As the sun sinks low,
And stars begin to gleam,
We wander hand in hand,
Into the night's dream.

Fleeting Fantasies

In the garden of dreams, we dance,
Whispers of wishes, a fleeting chance.
Silhouetted shadows in twilight's embrace,
Colors of hope in a soft, gentle space.

Winds of change carry stories untold,
Tender and fragile, a beauty to hold.
Moments like petals drift down from the sky,
Captured in memories as time wanders by.

With every heartbeat, a flicker, a spark,
Glimmers of magic unmasking the dark.
Ethereal echoes that stroke the night air,
A reverie born from a dreamer's own care.

Fleeting and fragile, yet bold in their quest,
These fantasies fade, but we'll hold them blessed.
In the hush of the evening, we make our retreat,
Carrying whispers of dreams bittersweet.

Nets of the Nocturne

Beneath a sky stitched with silver and gold,
Nets of the nocturne catch tales to be told.
Stars weave a tapestry, bright and so rare,
Casting their wishes in shimmering air.

Whispers of night wrap the world in a sigh,
Secrets unravel as the shadows fly.
Dreamers awaken, their hearts in a trance,
Caught in the magic of night's gentle dance.

The moon hums a lullaby soft and low,
Guiding the wanderers where shadows go.
Every flicker of light, a promise divine,
Enchanting the silence with delicate lines.

Veils of illusion float softly above,
Casting reflections of mystery and love.
In nets of the nocturne, our spirits ascend,
Finding new realms where the echoes don't end.

Spirits in the Loom

In the loom of the night, we weave our fate,
Threads of existence that never sedate.
Patterns emerging, a dance in the dark,
Spirits entwined leave an everlasting mark.

Whispers of time stitch our hearts with a thread,
Fables and dreams where the brave have tread.
Colors and shadows blend in a swirl,
Every encounter adds depth to our world.

With every heartbeat a new tale is spun,
Crafting connections beneath a warm sun.
Spirits of laughter, of sorrow, of joy,
In the fabric of life, we're wove to enjoy.

Every moment we share becomes part of the weave,
Treasures we gather, patterns we believe.
In the loom of existence, we find our design,
Creating the stories of love and of time.

Chasing Stardust

In the hush of the night, we chase after dreams,
Stardust a-glimmer, as bright as it seems.
Fleeting as whispers, elusive as light,
We dance with the cosmos, igniting the night.

Galaxies twinkle, calling our name,
We ride on the wings of a celestial flame.
With spirits alight, we traverse the vast,
Chasing the echoes of futures uncast.

Footprints of stardust map paths we can't see,
Leading us forward, wild and carefree.
The universe holds us in its embrace,
A canvas of wonder, our infinite space.

Lost in the beauty of twilight's soft glow,
Chasing the stardust where dreams dare to flow.
Together we'll journey, forever we'll roam,
In the heart of the cosmos, we've found our home.

Guardians of Slumber

In the twilight's gentle sigh,
Dreams gather, soft and nigh.
Stars shimmer in silent keep,
Guardians shield the world of sleep.

Whispers ride the moonlit breeze,
Tales of old drift through the trees.
With each heartbeat, shadows play,
Guiding souls till break of day.

Nestled in the night's cocoon,
Cradled tight by silver moon.
Rest, dear heart, let worries fade,
In this sacred serenade.

Veils of starlight softly weave,
Dreamers dance, and none bereave.
Close your eyes, let visions bloom,
Guardians watch, dispelling gloom.

On this path of dreams secure,
Find the peace that feels so pure.
In the arms of night's embrace,
Take your flight to endless space.

Night's Embrace

Beneath the cloak of velvet night,
The world finds peace, a soft delight.
With every breath, the shadows blend,
In tender hush, the day will end.

Stars awake, their laughter bright,
Painting the canvas, purest light.
Silvery beams through branches weave,
In night's embrace, we dare believe.

Crisp air hums a lullaby,
Moonbeams dance as owls glide by.
Every rustle, every sigh,
Whispers secrets from the sky.

Wrapped in dreams, the heart will soar,
In twilight's magic, we explore.
A symphony of gentle grace,
Each moment in night's warm embrace.

When dawn awakes with blush of gold,
The stories whispered shall be told.
Yet for now, let shadows nigh,
Cradle dreams until we fly.

The Enchanted Frame

In a frame of twinkling stars,
Timeless tales of fate are ours.
Every portrait, every hue,
Holds a secret just for you.

Whispers echo through the glass,
Memories of days that pass.
In the shadows, dreams abide,
Lost in the moments, deep inside.

Brush of wind and fleeting light,
In the frame, the world ignites.
Colors blend in tender streams,
Painting pathways made of dreams.

Time's caress, a gentle guide,
In this haven, hearts confide.
Open wide the enchanted door,
For within lies so much more.

So let the magic spill and shine,
In the frame, our lives entwine.
Captured moments, here they stay,
In the light, they dance and play.

Shadows of the Soul

In the quiet, whispers sigh,
Shadows linger, soft and shy.
Every heartbeat tells a tale,
In the dark where dreams prevail.

Through the night, the echoes call,
Ancient secrets rise and fall.
In the stillness, shadows dance,
Weaving patterns in a trance.

Hushed desires, hidden fears,
In the dim, release your tears.
Embrace the night, let go your pain,
Shadows whisper, you'll regain.

Tread softly in the moon's soft light,
Find the courage to take flight.
In the depths where shadows dwell,
There's a power that can compel.

Through the veil of night, behold,
The journey's worth, the brave and bold.
In shadows deep, the soul shall find,
A path to light, forever kind.

Mysteries in a Feathered Frame

In shadows cast by moonlit beams,
A whisper flutters through the night.
Feathers brush the edge of dreams,
Embracing truths hidden from sight.

Colors shift in twilight's glow,
Each feather holds a secret tale.
With every flutter, winds will blow,
Guiding souls on whispered sail.

A tapestry woven through the skies,
Each thread a memory lost,
The feathered whispers softly rise,
Leaving echoes of love's cost.

Bound by silence, winged and free,
The mystery deepens with the dawn.
In a world where shadows flee,
The truths remain, forever drawn.

So listen close, for nature speaks,
In every rustle, each soft sigh.
The heart discovers what it seeks,
In mysteries where dreams still lie.

Secrets of the Dream Weaver

In the quiet of the night's embrace,
A dream weaver spins her thread.
With gentle hands and delicate grace,
She paints the tales that dance in our head.

Luminous glimmers dart like stars,
In her loom, possibilities blend.
She gathers whispers from afar,
And mends the heart where thoughts suspend.

With colors bold and softest hues,
Each dream a fragment of our soul.
Into the depths, she gently moves,
Each secret revealing, making us whole.

Time is lost in this sacred place,
Where hope and fears freely entwine.
In the web of night, we chase,
The dreams that shimmer, infinite and fine.

Awakened in dawn's tender light,
We carry pieces of her art.
Each new day begins the flight,
Of dreams embedded in the heart.

The Twilight's Silent Vigil

In twilight's hush, the world stands still,
As shadows stretch and whispers weave.
A sentinel of time's soft chill,
The day begins to gently leave.

Beneath the stars, the night takes form,
As silence wraps the earth in peace.
A calming balm, a quiet warm,
Where secrets lay and worries cease.

The moon keeps watch with silver gaze,
While dreams unfurl like petals rare.
In this serene and sacred phase,
The heart finds solace in the air.

With every breath, a sacred bond,
Between the day and night's embrace.
In twilight's stillness, we respond,
To nature's most enduring grace.

Let every soul in twilight dwell,
And with the stars, their wishes share.
For in this hour, we know so well,
The night holds love's eternal flair.

Reflections from a Midnight Canvas

A canvas stretched beneath the sky,
Where dreams converge with midnight's glow.
Each brushstroke whispers a soft sigh,
In shadows deep, the colors flow.

Stars drip gently from the brush,
Each twinkle sparkles like a thought.
In this still hour, there's no rush,
Artistry born from battles fought.

The moon, a muse, casts silver light,
Illuminating tales untold.
In every shadow, hope takes flight,
With strokes of courage, fierce and bold.

Painted whispers in midnight's scheme,
Capture feelings both sweet and vast.
In this gallery of dreams,
Every heartbeat echoes from the past.

So let us dare to paint the night,
With colors bright and voices clear.
For in this canvas, pure delight,
We find a world beyond all fear.

The Web of Serene Visions

In tranquil dreams where shadows weave,
Silent whispers guide what we believe.
A tapestry of light takes flight,
Embracing hearts in soft moonlight.

Gentle breezes caress the mind,
Painting visions, warm and kind.
Each thread a story yet untold,
In silken hues of blue and gold.

The stars align in patterns rare,
As hopes unfurl in midnight air.
A dance of thoughts, a fleeting glance,
Lost in the art of sweet romance.

Through each sigh, the night unfolds,
A canvas bright with colors bold.
In every heartbeat, dreams arise,
In the web spun by silent skies.

We wander through this sacred place,
With every breath, our souls embrace.
In serene visions, we are found,
In whispered love, forever bound.

Dance of Ethereal Nightmares

In shadows dark where secrets hide,
The dance of fears we cannot bide.
Ethereal whispers creep and crawl,
Calling forth the echoes of our fall.

Figures flit in starlit gloom,
Chasing hopes through the silent room.
Twisted tales in moonlit dread,
Where once we soared, now we tread.

A haunting melody begins to play,
Waking dreams that drift away.
Specters swirl in a ghostly trance,
Weave their fate in a perilous dance.

Each turn a shiver, a broken light,
Lost in the labyrinth of the night.
Yet through the dark, we learn to fight,
Embrace the shadows, hold them tight.

In the depths where nightmares reign,
We find the strength to rise again.
With courage forged in midnight's fire,
We dance through darkness, never tire.

Echoes Beneath the Sky

Underneath the vast expanse,
Our voices merge in a quiet dance.
Memories linger, echoes of old,
In the silence, stories unfold.

Clouds drift by like whispered dreams,
Carrying hopes on sunlit beams.
Each echo shapes the world we know,
In twilight's glow, our spirits flow.

Beneath the stars, hearts intertwine,
In the stillness, love's design.
Fragments of laughter, soft and near,
Resonate, whispering what we fear.

Time stands still, a fleeting glance,
Wrapped in the warmth of chance romance.
As night descends on this sacred land,
We write our fate with each trembling hand.

In the echoes, our souls take flight,
Finding solace in the night.
Each heartbeat sings beneath the sky,
In harmony, we learn to fly.

Catching the Lullaby of Wishes

In twilight's hush, dreams softly sway,
Lullabies whisper at the end of day.
Wishes linger on a starry stream,
Carried forth on the wings of dreams.

Gentle notes in the evening air,
Wrap the world in a tender care.
Each sigh a wish, each breath a plea,
Catching moments, setting them free.

Moonlight laughs as shadows play,
Guiding hearts to a hopeful bay.
Every star a promise bright,
Resonating through the folds of night.

With every wish, our spirits soar,
Unlocking dreams behind closed doors.
In this lullaby, we find our way,
To light the path of another day.

So close your eyes, let your heart glide,
In the lullaby, forever reside.
Catching wishes as they arise,
Under the canvas of endless skies.

Pathways through the Starry Veil

Under the cosmic canopy bright,
Footsteps guided by the moon's light.
Winding trails of silver glow,
Whispers of dreams softly flow.

Stars above twinkle and gleam,
Carrying thoughts, a hidden theme.
Through the silence, wonders speak,
In this realm, the lost seek.

Galaxies swirl in the dark,
Each a story, a lingering spark.
The universe unfolds its lore,
Inviting hearts to explore.

Softly, the night wraps around,
In its breath, magic is found.
Traversing pathways, hand in hand,
We uncover the endless land.

Beneath the starry veil we tread,
With every step, a new thread.
In the tapestry of the night,
We find our way, guided by light.

Tales from the Feathered Horizon

Whispers ride the winds of flight,
Feathers dance with pure delight.
Stories carried on the breeze,
Echoing through the sacred trees.

Clouds drift slowly overhead,
Each a canvas, dreams are spread.
Songs of joy and loss entwined,
In the feathers, secrets bind.

Crests of mountains touch the sky,
Where the eagles soar and cry.
Their wings weave tales of old,
Of journeys vast, courageous and bold.

From their heights, the world looks small,
Yet from the ground, we hear their call.
Every rustle, a whispered plea,
In the horizon, we long to be.

In nature's arms, we find our place,
With the feathered creatures, we embrace.
Tales unfold in vibrant hues,
As the day turns to twilight blues.

Ensnared in Starlit Whispers

In the stillness of the night,
Voices echo, soft and light.
Words like shadows dance and play,
Under stars that guide the way.

Secrets shared with gentle grace,
In the dark, we find our space.
A caress of cosmic dreams,
In the silence, nothing seems.

Each glimmer tells a tale of old,
Of love and warmth, of hearts bold.
In the depths of night's embrace,
We trace the stars, we find our place.

Ensnared in whispers, we unite,
Together we chase the light.
In starlit realms, our spirits soar,
Forever longing to explore.

Bound by dreams and cosmic threads,
Where starlit whispers gently spread.
In each twinkle, a promise speaks,
Of adventures our heart seeks.

Murmurs of the Night's Embrace

In twilight's arms, the shadows grow,
Secrets linger, soft and slow.
Murmurs rise beneath the moon,
Carried far, a gentle tune.

Crickets chirp in harmony,
Nature's serenade sets us free.
The night unfolds its velvety wings,
As the world rests, the heart sings.

Starlight drapes the silent trees,
Caressing branches in the breeze.
A glow that beckons dreamers near,
To lose themselves without fear.

In the dark, we find our truth,
Each whisper brings back the youth.
The night's embrace, warm and tight,
Wraps us close, within its light.

Murmurs echo, soft and clear,
In the shadows, we draw near.
Together we dance in starlit grace,
In the night's warm, tender embrace.

Echoes of a Starlit Dream

Under the velvet sky's embrace,
Whispers of night begin to trace.
Stars hum softly, secrets unfold,
In the darkness, stories told.

Moonlight dances on the stream,
Carrying hopes of a distant dream.
With every twinkle, wishes soar,
Echoes linger forevermore.

In the silence, hearts entwine,
A cosmic waltz, a love divine.
Finding solace in the gleam,
Lost in sweet starlit theme.

Ghostly figures wade the night,
Guided gently by starlight.
Every shadow casts a tale,
In this dream, we shall not pale.

Through the echoes, time stands still,
Beneath the stars, we feel the thrill.
In each heartbeat, magic streams,
Forever caught in starlit dreams.

Woven Wishes

In a tapestry of time, we weave,
Threads of hope, dreams to believe.
Colors bright, with whispers sweet,
In every knot, our souls shall meet.

Sunrise paints the morning light,
Embroidered tales within our sight.
Every strand a wish we share,
Binding love in the open air.

A loom of laughter, a fabric of grace,
We find our joy in this sacred space.
With hands entwined, we craft the day,
Woven wishes guide our way.

Each moment stitched with gentle care,
In the heart's embrace, we find a prayer.
Through woven dreams, we dance, we play,
Together forever, come what may.

At twilight's end, the shadows stretch,
In hues of gold, our spirits fetch.
Woven wishes, a radiant seam,
In the night, we chase the dream.

Moonsong Reverie

In a realm where silence sighs,
Moonlight spills from sapphire skies.
Each note a soft and tender gleam,
We float within the nocturne dream.

Whispers of the night ignite,
Filling hearts with pure delight.
In rhythms deep like ocean tides,
A sacred song, where love abides.

Crickets strum a serenade,
While shadows dance in twilight's shade.
Every heartbeat, a gentle tone,
In this reverie, we're not alone.

Clouds drift softly, hooded grace,
As we find solace in this space.
Together lost in moonsong's charm,
Wrapped in night and love's warm arm.

As dawn approaches, we'll hold tight,
To echoes of our shared delight.
In dreams of silver, we'll remain,
Drifting softly through the rain.

Secrets in the Silk

Beneath the threads of softest sheen,
Lies a world that's yet unseen.
Whispers float on silken air,
Carrying dreams with tender care.

In twilight's hush, secrets bloom,
Woven gently, dispelling gloom.
Every fiber holds a trace,
Of hidden thoughts in soft embrace.

Each touch ignites a gentle spark,
In the twilight, chasing dark.
Wrapped in layers, tender and bold,
Stories of love and hearts unfold.

Silk dances lightly in the breeze,
Carried by the night's soft tease.
With every fold, a poem told,
Of yearning souls and dreams of gold.

In every stitch, a promise lies,
Glistening softly 'neath starry skies.
Secrets flutter on whispers sweet,
In the silk, our hearts shall meet.

Passages Through Night

In darkness deep, the shadows creep,
Whispers of dreams, where secrets keep.
Stars flicker soft, in a velvet sky,
Guiding lost souls, as time drifts by.

Veils of silence wrap the air,
Holding tight, a tranquil prayer.
Moonlight dances on the stream,
Finding solace in a fleeting dream.

Footsteps echo on the path unseen,
Through the woods, where few have been.
Breezes murmur through the trees,
Carrying tales of ancient seas.

Journey on, through the haze of night,
Chasing shadows, seeking light.
With each heartbeat, the world unfolds,
In whispered secrets, the night beholds.

As dawn approaches, the darkness fades,
Leaving behind the night's charades.
In gentle hues, the morning breaks,
Awakening dreams, as daylight wakes.

Sylvan Aspirations

In forests green, where echoes play,
Dreams arise with the break of day.
Leaves rustle softly, a tender sigh,
Whispers of hope in the branches high.

Beneath the boughs, the wildflowers sway,
Finding their strength in nature's way.
Sunbeams filter through the leaves,
Awakening hearts, where magic weaves.

A river flows with secrets old,
Tales of the earth and stories untold.
In quiet pools, reflections gleam,
Nurturing visions, feeding the dream.

Birds take flight, their spirits free,
Carving arcs across the canopy.
In every song, a promise glows,
A symphony where the spirit flows.

With each step on this hallowed ground,
The echoes of nature's love abound.
In sylvan realms, aspirations rise,
In harmony beneath the skies.

Ethereal Echoes

In whispered winds, the echoes soar,
Carrying tales from a distant shore.
Moonlit paths where phantoms glide,
In quiet realms, where dreams abide.

A fog descends, soft and light,
Wrapping the world in gentle night.
Through veils of mist, the visions call,
In ethereal realms, we dare to fall.

Stars twinkle, like eyes in the dark,
Guiding souls to where dreams embark.
With every heartbeat, the silence sings,
Binding the night with timeless strings.

In shadows deep, our fears unwind,
As we embrace what fate has aligned.
In fleeting moments, we find our grace,
In ethereal echoes, we trace our place.

For every sigh and every tear,
There lies a truth, both bright and clear.
Through silent passages, journeys reflect,
In the dance of the night, we connect.

Whispered Serenades

In twilight hours, soft tales unfold,
Melodies sweet, in whispers told.
The night air hums a tender song,
Embracing hearts where we belong.

Flickering candles cast shadows warm,
Cradling dreams in their gentle form.
With every note, the silence breaks,
Revealing magic in the paths it makes.

A lullaby floats on the breeze,
Weaving through branches, stirring the leaves.
In the distance, a voice calls clear,
A serenade that draws us near.

In quiet corners, our spirits intertwine,
Lost in the rhythm, a moment divine.
As stars awaken in the velvet space,
A symphony blooms, leaving no trace.

With every heartbeat, we surrender slow,
In whispered serenades, our love will grow.
For in the night's embrace, we find our way,
Together as one, until break of day.

Tales from Above

In skies so vast, where dreams reside,
Clouds drift gently, like thoughts untried.
Gentle whispers from the heights,
Stories woven in moonlit nights.

The sun dips low, painting the day,
Golden hues in a soft ballet.
Birds sing songs of freedom's flight,
Chasing shadows, kissing the light.

Stars awaken, one by one,
Tales of love from the night begun.
Each twinkle holds a secret dear,
Echoes of laughter, joy, and cheer.

Wisps of clouds in playful dance,
Taking dreams on a fleeting chance.
From up above, we learn to see,
The beauty of life's tapestry.

With every sunset comes a dawn,
Hope and wonder, forever drawn.
The tales from high will softly call,
Inviting hearts to rise and fall.

Whispered Shadows

In twilight's grasp, where shadows creep,
Secrets linger, soft and deep.
Whispers float on the evening breeze,
Carrying tales between the trees.

Moonlight dances on silver streams,
Casting spells, igniting dreams.
Figures sway in the gentle night,
Lost in worlds where wrong feels right.

Echoes linger, soft and clear,
Memories fade, yet stay so near.
Through whispered words, the heart will bind,
Finding solace in the mind.

Footsteps trace the path of yore,
Ghostly hints at life's great lore.
Each shadow tells a tale profound,
Of love and loss, always around.

As stars align and silence reigns,
The whispered shadows break the chains.
In darkness, light takes shape anew,
Revealing wonders, always true.

The Keeper's Embrace

In a world where time stands still,
The Keeper waits with steadfast will.
With open arms and heart so wide,
Inviting souls to gently glide.

Through seasons change, the Keeper stays,
Guarding dreams in a tender gaze.
With every breath, a story spun,
A journey shared, two hearts as one.

In moments fleeting, love takes flight,
The Keeper's warmth, a guiding light.
With every sigh, a promise made,
In shadowed paths, no need for shade.

Through laughter's joy and sorrow's tear,
The Keeper's voice remains so clear.
Echoing hopes, both big and small,
Embracing all, the keeper's call.

So seek the arms that hold your dreams,
In gentle streams where kindness gleams.
The Keeper whispers through each phase,
In tender love, forever stays.

Dancing with the Stars

Beneath the sky, where starlight glows,
A dance begins, as passion flows.
With every twirl, the world ignites,
Lost in rhythm of endless nights.

The moon looks on with a smile bright,
Guiding hearts in the soft twilight.
With arms outstretched, we chase the beams,
Floating free in our shared dreams.

Galaxies spin in celestial grace,
In this vast cosmic, timeless space.
A ballet of light, no end in sight,
Eclipsing shadows, igniting the night.

With twinkling eyes, we laugh and sing,
In the embrace of the love we bring.
Together we leap, together we soar,
In a dance forever adored.

As dawn approaches, the music slows,
Yet in our hearts, the memory grows.
We've danced with stars, we've felt the fire,
In cosmic love, our spirits aspire.

The Guardian's Wish

In shadows deep, the guardian waits,
A whisper of hope, while destiny fates.
With watchful eyes upon the night,
He weaves a dream, a flicker of light.

Ancient secrets in the breeze,
Glimmers of wisdom among the trees.
He guards the realm with steadfast grace,
A silent heart in a bustling place.

The moon may rise, obscured and shy,
Yet still he stands, he won't comply.
His wish unfurls like morning's bloom,
To banish despair, to elude the gloom.

As dawn approaches, colors blend,
A hopeful sigh, as night will end.
The guardian smiles, the world takes flight,
His wish now shared in morning light.

In every heart, his dreams reside,
A guardian's wish, forever bide.
In love's embrace, we find our way,
A brighter world, a brand new day.

Nightbound Stories

Beneath the stars, the ancients speak,
Of tales untold and mystique.
In the hush of dusk, they softly gleam,
Weaving whispers, a collective dream.

Moonbeams dance on paths once trod,
Where shadows linger, and hope is broad.
Each story falls like soothing rain,
Carving out joy amidst the pain.

The night unfolds like an open book,
With every glance, a secret look.
Each corner holds a different tale,
Of love and loss, of hearts that sail.

In starlit corners, we gather near,
Sharing our laughter, our joy, our fear.
A tapestry held within the night,
Bound by stories, our hearts alight.

So listen close as the night reveals,
The stories hidden, the truth that heals.
In shadows deep, let courage bloom,
For every heart's tale dispels the gloom.

A Tapestry of Sights

Through the fabric of time, moments flow,
Each thread a memory, hung in tow.
Vivid colors blend on high,
A masterpiece woven by the sky.

From dawn's first blush to dusk's embrace,
Nature's canvas finds its place.
Golden rays brush softly by,
Kissing the earth, a gentle sigh.

Waves crash down with rhythmic grace,
Mountains stand guard, a timeless face.
Fields of flowers sway and play,
A symphony of scents on display.

Stars emerge like diamonds bright,
Painting dreams upon the night.
In the stillness, behold the sights,
A vivid world where wonder ignites.

So tread softly, and take a glance,
In each moment lies a chance.
Life's tapestry, both rich and wide,
Holds beauty waiting, right outside.

Boughs of Slumber

Beneath the branches, shadows fall,
A quiet whisper, a slumber's call.
Cocooned in dreams, the world retreats,
Where peace settles and time discreet.

Softly cradled in nature's sigh,
The night enfolds, as stars comply.
Gentle breezes through leaves sweep,
Lullabies sung to those asleep.

In branches thick where secrets lie,
The moon peeks through, a watchful eye.
Each bough a guardian for the night,
Embracing all in tender light.

Awake, dear souls, in dreams we find,
The joys we seek, the ties that bind.
So let the night be a soothing balm,
In boughs of slumber, life feels calm.

As dawn arrives with golden hue,
From dreams we rise, to be anew.
But in our hearts, we'll carry still,
The tranquil night, the silent thrill.

Veils of Illusion

In shadows cast by flickering light,
We wander through the endless night.
A whisper soft, a haunting sound,
In hidden truths, we're tightly bound.

Mirages dance in our weary minds,
As dreams and reality intertwine.
Each breath concealed, a secret kept,
In veils of illusion, quietly crept.

The heart plays tricks in dim-lit halls,
Where every echo gently calls.
We chase the silhouettes of time,
Veils of illusion, silent rhyme.

Yet through the fog, a glimpse appears,
A fleeting face that draws our tears.
A tether strong, a fragile thread,
In veils of illusion, hope is fed.

So hold on tight, don't slip away,
For in the haze, the spirits sway.
Between the lines of what is real,
Veils of illusion, we can feel.

The Fabric of Sleep

In twilight's grip, the world slows down,
A gentle hush, no need for sound.
We drift on clouds, a soft embrace,
The fabric of sleep, a sacred space.

Dreams stitch together night and day,
In quiet corners, shadows play.
With every thread, a story spun,
The fabric of sleep, where all is one.

Slumbering whispers, secrets shared,
In every heart's beat, love declared.
Wrapped in warmth, a soft cocoon,
The fabric of sleep, our soft tune.

Awake to find the dawn's first light,
Yet hold the dreams within your sight.
A tapestry of hope unfurls,
The fabric of sleep, our hidden pearls.

As night descends, we'll weave anew,
With stars above and skies so blue.
Embrace the night, let worries steep,
In the gentle fold of the fabric of sleep.

Shimmers of Memory

In the quiet, echoes softly gleam,
Shimmers of memory, like a dream.
Fleeting moments, bright as the sun,
In the heart's chamber, they still run.

Fragments flicker, a visual song,
In the tapestry of where we belong.
Each laugh recalled, each tear that fell,
Shimmers of memory weave their spell.

Through the corridors of yesteryear,
Wisps of laughter, traces of fear.
In every glance, a tale to tell,
Shimmers of memory, deep as a well.

Time may fade, but spirits stay,
In the dance of shadows, they play.
A whisper soft, a guiding bell,
Shimmers of memory, cast their spell.

So close your eyes, and let it flow,
Through woven threads of long ago.
In the light of dawn, we'll find our key,
Shimmers of memory, setting us free.

Night's Canvas

Upon the canvas, stars are strewn,
A silent lullaby, a whispering tune.
Each brush of night, a tale unfolds,
In hues of dreams, the cosmos holds.

Moonlight spills, a silver flow,
On hidden paths and fields below.
In shadows painted, mysteries bloom,
Night's canvas, a magical room.

Beneath the veil of twilight's sigh,
The universe dances, we wonder why.
In every stroke, a heartbeat's might,
On night's canvas, we find our light.

As dawn approaches, colors blend,
In the soft embrace, we find an end.
Yet in our hearts, the echoes stay,
On night's canvas, where dreams play.

So take a moment, breathe it in,
Let night's canvas your soul fill.
In every star, a memory lives,
A masterpiece that always gives.

Whispers of Woven Stars

In the quiet of the night,
Stars begin to sing,
Softly weaving tales,
Of dreams that nighttime brings.

A tapestry of light,
Adorned with silver beams,
They dance in cosmic flight,
Guiding our sweetest dreams.

Whispers of the cosmos,
Cradle the weary mind,
In their gentle glow,
Hope and peace we find.

Each twinkle tells a story,
Of worlds beyond our sight,
Inviting us to wander,
Through the endless night.

So let your heart take wing,
On the fabric of the sky,
For in the stars' embrace,
We learn how to fly.

Shadows in the Moonlight

Beneath the watchful eye,
The moon casts a soft glow,
Where shadows softly play,
And secrets start to flow.

Whispers of the night breeze,
Carry tales untold,
Shadowy figures dance,
In this realm of gold.

Rustling leaves, a secret,
In the twilight's embrace,
As time begins to linger,
In this ethereal space.

Night wraps the world in silk,
With stars that gently gleam,
In the hush of the dark,
Reality feels like a dream.

Find solace in the dark,
Where shadows softly blend,
In moonlight's tender grace,
We discover and transcend.

Threads of Night's Embrace

In the fabric of the night,
Dreams are stitched with care,
Each thread a whispered wish,
Floating in the air.

A gentle lullaby plays,
As stars begin to weave,
The fabric of our hopes,
In which we choose to believe.

Softly wrapped in twilight,
We drift as night descends,
Finding peace in shadows,
Where the day quietly ends.

Threads of silver moonlight,
Knit together our fears,
As night's embrace enfolds,
Washing away the tears.

So let us dream together,
In this quiet, sacred space,
For in the threads of night,
We find a warm embrace.

Guardians of Slumbering Dreams

In the realms of silent night,
Guardians softly tread,
Watching over slumber,
As we drift in our bed.

With every breath we take,
They whisper ancient lore,
Guiding us through the veil,
To realms we've not explored.

Starlight forms their lanterns,
While shadows keep them near,
In this dance of dreams,
We shed our waking fear.

Each moment's gentle passage,
Is cradled in their grace,
They carry our desires,
In the night's warm embrace.

Let their watchful presence,
Guide our journey deep,
For in their peaceful shadows,
We find our dreams to keep.

The Midnight Weave

In whispers thick as midnight mist,
We gather threads, an ancient twist.
Each stitch a dream, a silent plea,
In shadows deep, we weave to see.

With fingers dance, the loom awake,
Patterns formed for love's sweet sake.
A tapestry of heart and soul,
In twilight's glow, we make it whole.

Beneath the stars, our secrets spin,
As time eludes, the night begins.
Each fleeting hour, a strand of light,
Together bound, we soar and fight.

The midnight calls, our spirits soar,
In woven threads, forevermore.
Through tangled paths, we find our way,
In fabric soft, our dreams will stay.

So let us weave till dawn's embrace,
In whispered tales, we find our place.
A world of magic, bright and bold,
In midnight's weave, our fate unfolds.

Fragments of the Mind

Scattered pieces on the floor,
Thoughts and whispers, evermore.
In silence lost, I seek to find,
The shattered glass of my own mind.

Memories cling like morning dew,
Fleeting glimpses, shadows too.
Each fragment calls, a voice unknown,
In quiet corners, I walk alone.

A puzzle formed of loss and gain,
In every shard, a hint of pain.
Yet from the wreckage, light will spill,
In chaos graced by strength of will.

Reflections dance in flickered light,
As day succumbs to fading night.
With every piece, I learn to see,
The beauty found in fractured me.

So gather scraps from every space,
And hold them close, embrace their grace.
A mind once broken, now defined,
In every bit, a life aligned.

A Dance of Shadows

In twilight's glow, the shadows play,
They twist and swirl, then fade away.
With every step, a story told,
In silence bold, the night unfolds.

A gentle breeze ignites the night,
Whispers shared in soft moonlight.
We move as one, in silence deep,
A dance of shadows, secrets keep.

With every turn, we leave behind,
The weight of hopes, the ties that bind.
In harmony, we find our peace,
As troubles wane, our fears release.

The rhythm flows beneath our feet,
A silent hymn, both raw and sweet.
In every sway, a spark ignites,
A dance of shadows in the night.

So hold me close, let shadows weave,
In fleeting moments, we believe.
A dance that calls us to explore,
In shadows deep, we seek for more.

Entwined Fates

In quiet threads our fates entwine,
A tapestry of yours and mine.
With every heartbeat, closer drawn,
In whispered dreams, we greet the dawn.

Through winding paths, we share our fears,
In laughter bright, in silent tears.
Each moment stitched, a bond so tight,
In shadowed dusk, in morning light.

A dance of steps, a careful sway,
In every choice, we find our way.
Through storm and calm, we brave the tide,
In love's embrace, we stand with pride.

With hands held fast, we face the night,
In woven fates, our hearts take flight.
No distance wide can break the thread,
In every word, our promise said.

So here we stand, forever near,
In every laugh, in every tear.
Entwined we stay, come what may,
In the dance of fate, we find our way.

Whispers in the Twilight

In twilight's glow, soft echoes play,
The fleeting dreams of light's decay.
A gentle breeze, a tender sigh,
Where shadows dance and laughter lie.

Stars blink awake, a silent choir,
As night unfolds its deep desire.
With every breath, the world slows down,
And whispers weave through twilight's gown.

The moon ascends, a golden sphere,
Illuminating all that's dear.
In hushed tones, the night takes flight,
Embracing all with pure delight.

Beneath the trees, their branches sway,
As secrets linger, softly lay.
With every rustle, stories form,
In twilight's arms, the heart feels warm.

The final light, a fading gleam,
As night unveils its daring dream.
With whispers wrapped in velvet's seam,
We journey forth, a shared theme.

Threads of Ethereal Night

In the quiet, stars align,
Weaving tales in threads divine.
Each shimmer holds a story true,
Illuminating paths we knew.

Veils of darkness softly sway,
Embracing dreams that drift away.
In absence, stillness starts to bloom,
While shadows dance around the room.

A gentle hush, the night exhales,
As whispered winds weave secret tales.
In every heart, a spark ignites,
Connecting souls through endless nights.

Softly woven, starlit beams,
Reality blurs with our dreams.
In this realm, we float in flight,
As time dissolves in ethereal night.

The moonlight threads through branches bare,
Casting spells upon the air.
Each glimmer holds a promise bright,
Binding us in this cosmic light.

Captured Visions

In silent frames, the moments freeze,
Captured visions ride the breeze.
Through fleeting glances, we can see,
The fleeting dance of you and me.

Polaroid hearts in vibrant hue,
Each snapshot tells a story true.
Time is etched in shades of gold,
A treasure trove of tales retold.

In every image, laughter gleams,
The echo of our whispered dreams.
Frozen smiles, emotions bright,
Hold magic in the softest light.

Memories wrap like ribbons tight,
Every glance, a spark of light.
With every moment, magic spins,
In captured visions, love begins.

As dusk gives way to moonlit grace,
Time stands still in this embrace.
A canvas bright with life's demand,
In captured visions, hand in hand.

Weaving the Unseen

With threads of hope, we start to weave,
The unseen tales that hearts conceive.
In silent moments, dreams entwine,
Creating worlds both yours and mine.

Through fabric soft, our secrets lie,
In whispered tones, we gently sigh.
Each stitch a promise, strong and true,
In patterns rich, we'll find our view.

The loom of fate is ever kind,
Tapestries of love combined.
In shadows deep, the colors blend,
As time unravels, we transcend.

With every breath, the magic's spun,
In this creation, we are one.
The unseen threads begin to show,
As destinies in silence flow.

As daylight fades, the night unveils,
The woven dreams that never fail.
In this embrace, the mystery's key,
We'll find the truth that sets us free.

Eldritch Dreams

In shadows deep, the whispers call,
A tapestry where nightmares sprawl.
Through mists of time, I wander lost,
Each dream a net, each thought a cost.

Beneath the gaze of ancient eyes,
Where cosmic secrets quietly rise.
I dance with phantoms, fluid, free,
In realms of dark, my mind doth see.

The stars align with eerie grace,
In realms beyond our known embrace.
A shiver runs through hallowed ground,
Where hidden things are tightly bound.

With every breath, reality bends,
And sanity begins to end.
I chase the echoes of my fears,
As truth dissolves in shadowed tears.

What lies ahead, I cannot tell,
In dreams that weave a silent spell.
I drift through night, my spirit soared,
In dreams once lost, now darkly stored.

Lanterns of the Spirit

In twilight's glow, we search for light,
Lanterns guide us through the night.
A flicker here, a whisper there,
Spirits linger, delicate air.

Each flame a wish, a hope reborn,
Illuminating paths forlorn.
In shadows deep where lost souls tread,
The lanterns shine where others dread.

A dance of flickers, soft and bright,
They weave a tale of ancient plight.
Let every lantern tell its truth,
Of sacred bonds and fleeting youth.

In every heart, a flame may dwell,
A beacon through the wishing well.
Together we rise, a band of light,
Lanterns guiding towards the right.

With every step, the darkness wanes,
And in our hearts, the spirit reigns.
Together we walk, hand in hand,
Through midnight's veil, our dreams will stand.

Veiled Horizons

Beyond the veil, horizons call,
Mysteries whispered, one and all.
Layers of light, shadows conspire,
A distant glimpse of worlds afire.

Invisible threads weave through the dark,
As visions flicker, leave their mark.
The edge of night, where dreams entwine,
Veiled horizons, silently shine.

In every mist, an echo aches,
Of distant lives and heartaches.
We reach for stars that seem so near,
Yet in their glow, we face our fear.

Beneath the cloak of timeless skies,
The unknown beckons, never lies.
Awakened souls, we search and seek,
To glimpse the truth, though faint and weak.

With every breath, the horizon bends,
In veils of time, the journey mends.
A dance of fate beneath the planes,
Through veiled horizons, love remains.

The Fabric of Nightmares

Woven threads of midnight's dread,
In silken knots, our fears are fed.
Each nightmare spun, a tale to tell,
In shadows, where the phantoms dwell.

A tapestry of lost regret,
Entangled hearts in dark offset.
Each thread reflects a haunting face,
In the fabric of the human race.

In whispers soft, the darkness calls,
As blood-red echoes fill the halls.
With every seam, a story grows,
In every tear, the anguish flows.

Yet in this weave, the strength resides,
For from the dark, the spirit hides.
A tapestry of light and night,
Through endless seams, we find our fight.

So rest, dear soul, in dreams unspun,
For in the dark, our hearts outrun.
The fabric holds our hopes so dear,
As nightmares fade, we rise, no fear.

Interwoven Echoes

Whispers dance upon the breeze,
Memories intertwine with trees.
In shadows deep, their tales unfold,
Stories ancient, softly told.

Echoes of laughter fill the air,
Every heartbeat, a timeless care.
Moments caught in fleeting sight,
Shimmer like stars in the quiet night.

Woven threads, both bright and dim,
Each voice weaves a sacred hymn.
From distant past to now and here,
Symphonies arise, crystal clear.

In corners lost, they softly shine,
Past and present, so divine.
Carried forth on life's sweet song,
In harmony, where we belong.

Together we breathe, the echoes blend,
Time suspended, hearts unbend.
In woven silence, we find peace,
A tapestry of love's release.

Veils of Reverie

In twilight's grasp, dreams take flight,
Hushed whispers blend with fading light.
Veils of reverie softly fall,
Painting secrets on the wall.

Tender visions dance in play,
Guiding thoughts that drift away.
On silver wings, the night unfolds,
Stories wrapped in starlit folds.

Gentle breezes breathe the truth,
Tracing paths of lost sweet youth.
In silent echoes, hearts will chase,
The fleeting shadows of their grace.

In distant realms, the spirits soar,
Across the vast and endless shore.
Each sigh a promise, softly shared,
In hearts where dreams are always aired.

Embrace the night, the dreamers call,
Wrapped in reveries, we are all.
In this stillness, our souls entwine,
A subtle bond that feels divine.

Celestial Guardians

Stars above in endless watch,
Celestial guardians, time will notch.
With every twinkle, wisdom speaks,
Guiding light for lost and meek.

In velvet skies, they gently glow,
Shimmering secrets, they bestow.
From ancient lore to hopes anew,
Shining paths that lead us through.

Galaxies swirl, a dance of fate,
Balanced whispers that never wait.
Each constellation, stories bold,
Of battles fought and dreams retold.

When darkness falls, they lend their light,
Encouraging souls to take flight.
For in their gaze, we find our way,
Through shadows deep, into the day.

Together we sail on cosmic streams,
Carried forth on tethered dreams.
In unity, we rise and shine,
Celestial guardians, forever divine.

Pathways of the Night

Beneath the moon's soft, silver glow,
Pathways of the night unfold slow.
In whispered dreams, the world transforms,
As shadows weave in gentle swarms.

Footsteps linger on the floor,
Guided by stars and tales of yore.
Each corner turned, a story spun,
In the embrace of the night's fun.

Luminous trails beckon the brave,
To dance with winds, the heart to pave.
In the silence, secrets lie,
Waiting for those who dare to try.

As night unfolds its velvet cloak,
Every breath a promise spoke.
Through woven paths of dark and light,
We trace our dreams until the light.

Together we wander, hand in hand,
On pathways drawn in starlit sand.
Every heartbeat, a gentle call,
In the night's cradle, we find our all.

Notes on the Breeze

Whispers of the leaves, so light,
Dancing in the golden light.
Songs of nature, soft and clear,
Carried gently, far and near.

Clouds drift slowly, dreams take flight,
Kisses of the sun ignite.
Every moment, fleeting grace,
Caught within a warm embrace.

Echoes of the world's sweet sound,
In harmony, we are bound.
Listen closely, hear the call,
Nature's symphony for all.

Breezes weave through fields of gold,
Tales of joy and love retold.
From the earth, a soft perfume,
Life and beauty start to bloom.

As the day begins to fade,
Stars awaken, softly laid.
In the night, our hopes arise,
Floating gently through the skies.

Flickers of Twilight

In the hush of fading light,
Colors blend, a wondrous sight.
Whispers of the coming night,
Painting dreams in soft twilight.

Crickets sing their evening songs,
As the world hums all along.
Shadows dance on paths so clear,
Inviting us to draw near.

Stars begin to sparkle bright,
Guiding hearts with gentle light.
Memories float on evening air,
Lingering with love and care.

Night unfolds its velvet cloak,
Hidden dreams and thoughts provoke.
Each flicker holds a tale to tell,
In this magic, all is well.

With each sigh, the moments pause,
Nature's beauty earns our applause.
In twilight's embrace, we find,
A gentle peace, a quiet mind.

Guardians of the Night

In the shadows, watchful eyes,
Guardians hidden, wise and wise.
With the moon's soft, silver glow,
They protect what we don't know.

Owls call softly, wings in flight,
Guardians of the velvet night.
Stars whisper secrets to the trees,
Carried forth by gentle breeze.

Midnight's cloak envelops all,
Nature's heartbeat, soft and small.
Listen closely, hear their song,
In this realm, we all belong.

Mysteries unfold above,
In harmony with peace and love.
Every creature, large and small,
Shares a part, plays a role in all.

Through the night, the spirits glide,
With their strength, we can confide.
Guardians watch from realms unseen,
In their presence, we are keen.

An Odyssey of Dreams

In the realm where shadows play,
We embark on thoughts, astray.
Each dream a path we must explore,
Unlocking tales forevermore.

Stars above invite our gaze,
Guiding us through midnight's haze.
Wonders stretch beyond our sight,
In the depths of endless night.

Voices whisper, calling clear,
Every heartbeat drawing near.
Journey forth through realms of thought,
Where the battles of dreams are fought.

Colors swirl in vibrant streams,
Crafting beauty from our dreams.
Every heartbeat marks a turn,
Lessons met, and passions learned.

As the dawn begins to break,
We awaken, dreams to take.
In the light, we see the way,
The odyssey keeps us at bay.

Chasing Dreamscapes

In twilight's glow, we race and fly,
Through fields where starlit wishes lie.
With every gasp, our spirits soar,
Chasing dreams that we adore.

Across the hills, the shadows dance,
In vibrant realms, we take our chance.
With laughter bright and hearts ablaze,
We wander on through night's soft haze.

The moonlight paints a silver stream,
Each fleeting moment, a whispered dream.
In the stillness, we hear the call,
A secret voice that binds us all.

Beneath the stars, our hopes ignite,
A tapestry woven through the night.
With every step, new paths we find,
Chasing dreamscapes, hearts entwined.

As dawn begins to break our flight,
We hold the magic, pure and bright.
In every heartbeat, in every sigh,
The dreams we chased will never die.

Mysteries in the Loom

In shadows deep, a secret spins,
The fabric of life, where the tale begins.
Threads of silver, gold, and blue,
Woven whispers speak anew.

Patterns form in the silent night,
Mysteries kept from our sight.
Each twist and turn, a story told,
In the loom, the threads unfold.

Time weaves close, then drifts away,
In intricate designs, we sway.
A dance of fate, a cosmic rhyme,
Each stitch binds us closer in time.

The weaver's hands, both skilled and wise,
Capture dreams through tender ties.
We follow paths of hidden lore,
Seeking truths forevermore.

As dawn arrives, we gaze in awe,
At the tapestry, forever raw.
In every hue, a legacy shines,
Mysteries in the loom divine.

Nightbloom's Secret

In the garden where shadows creep,
A nightbloom blooms where secrets sleep.
With petals soft like whispered sighs,
It beckons forth with mystic eyes.

The moonlight bathes its gentle form,
In silence deep, a tranquil storm.
What tales it holds, we long to hear,
In every petal, a spark of fear.

Underneath the starry shroud,
Ancient wisdom, softly loud.
Each fragrance holds a world unknown,
In nightbloom's heart, the light is sown.

We gather close and lean to see,
The stories sung, the wild decree.
In the stillness, a promise gleams,
Unlocking all our hidden dreams.

As dawn approaches, shadows fade,
The nightbloom's secrets gently wade.
In morning light, they drift away,
Till night returns to dance and sway.

Silken Whispers

In the twilight's hush, secrets weave,
Soft as shadows, hearts believe.
Silken whispers call the moon,
In gentle tones, they sing a tune.

Beneath the stars' watchful gaze,
Promises echo through the haze.
With every breath, a story spun,
In silver threads, our hearts are won.

The night unfurls its dark embrace,
Where dreams and wishes find their place.
In whispered vows, we dare to trust,
In silken bonds, we rise, we gust.

With every moment, time stands still,
Desires linger, softly thrill.
Through veils of night, our voices blend,
In silken whispers, love won't end.

As dawn approaches, gently bright,
We hold the magic of the night.
In every sigh, a lover's grace,
Silken whispers, time can't erase.

Fragments of Forgotten Dreams

In shadows cast by whispered sighs,
Fragments dance beneath the skies.
Echoes of laughter, faint and low,
Scattered memories in twilight's glow.

Petals drift on a gentle breeze,
Carrying tales of lost unease.
Each flutter holds a story untold,
Woven in fabric of dreams of old.

Stars wink down with knowing smiles,
Guiding the heart through winding miles.
In the silence, a voice may rise,
Awakening truth beneath the lies.

Time unfurls its delicate hand,
Guiding footsteps on shifting sand.
With each grain that slips away,
Fragments linger, refusing to sway.

Bright horizons beckon with grace,
Promises whispered to embrace.
In the night, let hope take flight,
Transforming fragments into light.

A Symphony of Shimmering Hope

In the dawn, soft notes arise,
Painting colors across the skies.
Melodies whisper, gentle and bright,
A symphony born from the night.

Harmonies linger in the air,
Dancing lightly, free from care.
Each chord is woven with dreams anew,
Shimmering hopes in vibrant hue.

Through valleys low and mountains high,
The sound of laughter fills the sky.
Every heartbeat, a rhythmic sound,
In this symphony, love is found.

When shadows fall and darkness calls,
The music lifts, and courage installs.
With every note, we rise and soar,
Together we'll reach for something more.

In every silence, a promise lies,
A shimmering hope that never dies.
With open hearts, we choose to believe,
In the symphony that we weave.

Lullabies Caught in Time

Moonlight bathes the world in peace,
As every worry finds release.
Softly sung in gentle rhyme,
Lullabies caught in endless time.

Crickets chirp their nightly tune,
Hushed whispers wrap the silver moon.
Dreamers drift on cloud-like streams,
Cradled within the heart of dreams.

Stars in stillness twinkle bright,
Guiding souls through velvet night.
In each breath, a soothing balm,
Awakening night's tender calm.

Time stands still in sacred space,
Every heartbeat finds its place.
Wrapped in warmth, the world takes flight,
In lullabies of soft twilight.

Close your eyes, let worries slide,
In the hush where dreams reside.
Caught in time, these whispers chime,
Embracing love within the rhyme.

The Keeper of Slumber's Secrets

A figure draped in twilight's mist,
Watches dreams, a timeless twist.
Guardian of slumber's sacred lore,
Unlocking secrets forevermore.

With gentle hands, they cradle night,
Guiding souls to realms of light.
Every whisper, a cherished tale,
Invisible paths where spirits sail.

Through veils of dreams, they softly tread,
Listening close to thoughts unsaid.
The keeper's gaze, both wise and kind,
Binds the threads of heart and mind.

In chaos found beneath the eyes,
They weave comfort with lullabies.
In slumber's arms, all fears must cease,
Resting in the keeper's peace.

Awake in dreams where silence sings,
The keeper breathes, and magic springs.
Holding tight to winter's gleam,
They are the weaver of the dream.

Harvesting Dreams

In fields where wishes grow bright,
We gather hope under the light.
Each whisper winds through golden grain,
Harvesting dreams from joy and pain.

The moon watches over our toil,
As hearts and hands mix with the soil.
Beneath the stars our visions bloom,
Creating magic amid the gloom.

With every seed that's placed with care,
A chance to soar, a chance to dare.
In these moments, life feels right,
We chase our dreams through day and night.

The wind carries laughter so sweet,
As we dance to a hopeful beat.
Our spirits rise with the dawn's embrace,
In this sacred, enchanting space.

Together we weave a tapestry,
Of dreams entwined in harmony.
Each thread a story, each stitch a vow,
Harvesting dreams, in this moment now.

Celestial Snare

Beneath a blanket of stars we lay,
Whispers of night guide our stray.
In the hush, a promise so near,
Caught in the snares of dreams sincere.

Galaxies spin in a cosmic dance,
Fate entwined in a fleeting chance.
We navigate through shadows and light,
The celestial pulls, our spirits ignite.

Like meteors tracing vibrant trails,
We reach for the heavens with hopes that sail.
In the vastness we find our way,
Celestial snare, where hearts dare play.

Each heartbeat echoes in cosmic rhyme,
Lost in the currents of space and time.
With every breath, a galaxy born,
In this vast expanse, we are reborn.

Stars whisper secrets, soft and low,
A timeless bond in the twilight glow.
Together we bask in the lunar glare,
Bound forever, in this celestial snare.

Echoing Horizons

Across the valley where sunbeams kiss,
Echoes of laughter wrap in bliss.
Horizons stretch with colors bold,
Tales of adventure waiting to unfold.

The mountains stand with stories grand,
In every shadow, dreams are planned.
The whispering winds, a gentle guide,
Echoing tales from the world outside.

With each step, we chase the unknown,
Fields of hope wait to be sown.
The horizon calls, a beckoning song,
As we journey forward, where we belong.

In the distance, the sun starts to rise,
Painting the sky with fire-tipped skies.
Every echo, a call to explore,
Horizons await; there's always more.

Together we roam through valleys wide,
With hearts ablaze and spirits high.
In every echo, we find our way,
To horizons bright, come what may.

Enigma of the Night

In shadows deep where secrets lie,
The night unveils a whispered sigh.
Stars above like jewels aglow,
Guard the dreams we dare to know.

Mysterious paths adorned in mist,
Hold the wonders we can't resist.
A symphony plays in silence profound,
In the enigma, the lost are found.

The moon's soft glow, a guiding light,
Illuminates the dance of night.
In realms unknown, we find our peace,
As time drifts on, our voices cease.

The whispers of fate weave in and out,
A riddle wrapped in shadows, no doubt.
With each moment, the night unfolds,
An enigma cherished, a story told.

In the stillness, our hearts will soar,
As we embrace what lies in store.
The enigma of the night shall reign,
Forever caught in this sweet refrain.

Lullabies of the Web

In the silence of the night,
Soft whispers spin and weave,
Gentle threads of dreams take flight,
Cradle thoughts, let minds believe.

Moonlight strokes the silver screen,
Dancing shadows, light and dark,
In the web, the dreams unseen,
Guide the dreamers, spark the spark.

Echoes hum in twilight's breath,
A lullaby to calm the soul,
Binding hearts and thoughts in depth,
In the web, we lose control.

Stars are strewn across the sky,
Like wishes caught in gentle nets,
As the night begins to sigh,
In this realm, no more regrets.

Cradle your dreams, let them flow,
In the web of twilight's charm,
Where the spirit's whispers grow,
In peaceful night, there's no harm.

Dreams Entangled

In the tapestry of night,
Visions twirl and intertwine,
Caught in threads of pure delight,
Chasing shadows, sipping wine.

Colors blend in soft embrace,
Every heartbeat weaves a tale,
Lost in time and sacred space,
Where the fleeting minds prevail.

Midnight whispers call us near,
In the fog of dreams, we sink,
Floating softly, void of fear,
Guided by a silver link.

Beneath the stars, our hopes align,
From the darkness, light is spun,
In the dreamscape, we all shine,
United in the quest for fun.

With each dawn, the visions part,
Yet in dreams, forever stay,
Through the night, we guard our heart,
In the dance of night and day.

Dances of the Mind

Thoughts like streams of silver grace,
Flow and twist in rhythmic beat,
In the silence, we find space,
As our heart and soul compete.

Chasing flickers of the new,
Every moment a ballet,
In the mind, the world's in view,
Where the visions gently sway.

Echoes of a distant day,
Whispers pull us in their wake,
Dancing shadows lead the way,
Through reflection, we are awake.

Memories like petals fall,
Scattering dreams upon the floor,
In the rhythm, we hear the call,
Letting go, we seek for more.

In the dance of thoughts, we thrive,
Curating dreams both bold and meek,
Through the strife, we learn to strive,
As the mind's embrace we seek.

Serenity's Net

Caught in nature's gentle weave,
Calmness drapes the evening air,
In silence, the heart believes,
And finds refuge, peace to share.

Twilight whispers to the sky,
Crickets serenade the night,
Underneath the stars, we lie,
In serenity's soft light.

Each breath sings a tranquil tune,
Moonlit paths of silken grace,
In the warmth of love's cocoon,
A sacred, timeless embrace.

Tangled dreams and hopes unite,
In this haven, pure and bright,
Every moment feels just right,
As we drift to endless night.

With each heartbeat, we connect,
In the web of love's intent,
Guided by what we reflect,
In serenity, time is spent.

The Soothsayer's Web

In shadows cast by whispering light,
The soothsayer spins tales of the night.
Each thread a vision, each knot a fate,
In the woven web, destinies wait.

Silent tongues of ancient lore,
In every corner, secrets implore.
The future dances in her palms,
A haunting song, a spell that calms.

Eyes like lanterns, wide and bright,
Glimmers of truth in the depths of night.
With trembling hands, she charts the stars,
Mapping the world through dreams and scars.

A flickering flame, a candle's glow,
Guiding lost souls where shadows flow.
In her embrace, fate softly bends,
And time surrenders, as night descends.

In the twilight's veil, her whispers swell,
Each prophecy penned, a haunting spell.
With every breath, the web grows tight,
A tapestry rich in the fabric of night.

Echoing Silhouettes

In the forest deep where shadows play,
Echoing silhouettes drift away.
The moonlight dances on leaves so shy,
Whispers of secrets in the night sky.

Figures collide in a timeless chase,
Fleeting forms with a ghostly grace.
Every rustle, a call from the past,
Every echo, a memory cast.

Footsteps linger on paths unknown,
In silken silence, truth is sown.
Lonely hearts in the dark unite,
Craving the warmth of forgotten light.

With each heartbeat, the night expands,
Fingers tracing ancient sands.
A journey begins with a flickering spark,
On the edge of reason, lost in the dark.

Together they dance, the shadows entwine,
In a world where the stars align.
Echoing softly through time's endless loop,
In a symphony of the silent group.

Fables of the Dreamworld

In realms where the wildest dreams are spun,
Fables whisper under the setting sun.
Clouds take shape, like stories untold,
In the heart of night, magic unfolds.

With silver threads, the weavers create,
Tales of wonder, of love, and fate.
The starlit sky, a canvas so wide,
Invites the lost souls to take a ride.

Every creature, a fragment of lore,
Dancing lightly on mythical shores.
They share their secrets in twilight's haze,
In the land of dreams, where time decays.

Through mystical forests and rivers that sing,
The heart leaps forth, on ethereal wings.
Each fable a key to unlock the delight,
In the dreamworld's embrace, we find our light.

With echoes of laughter, the night unfurls,
Fables spin round in enchanted swirls.
Closer we come to the softly gleamed,
Tales of the heart that forever beamed.

A Symphony of Slumber

In the hush of night, a lullaby plays,
Gentle whispers weave through the haze.
Stars like notes in a vast, dark sea,
Compose a melody, setting dreams free.

Pillows become clouds, soft and light,
Cradling the weary until morning's bright.
Each sigh a chord, a sweet, soft sound,
In slumber's embrace, tranquility found.

Waves of sleep wash over the land,
Painting visions with a soothing hand.
Drifting through valleys of muted gray,
Where the heart and mind can softly sway.

In slumber's grip, time bends and sways,
A symphony hums on moonlit highways.
Every heartbeat a rhythm, gentle and pure,
In the symphony of slumber, we find allure.

As dawn approaches, dreams softly fade,
Yet the echoes of night in our hearts invade.
A lingering song that forever hums,
In the quiet of dawn, the new day drums.

www.ingramcontent.com/pod-product-compliance
Ingram Content Group UK Ltd.
Pitfield, Milton Keynes, MK11 3LW, UK
UKHW030907221224
452712UK00007B/812